Amarozi Creations

Chicago, Illinois

Dedication

This book is dedicated to our fellow writer, Yvonne S. Finley, the motivating force behind the creation of this book. Doing this project brought together two of her passions.

Her commitment to writing and sharing her words inspired this unique writing collaboration. Yvonne loved writing and books, and her friends were often rewarded with books she purchased expressly for them.

Sadly, Yvonne made her transition after a sudden illness in May 2022 at age 85. She was excited that Three Writers and an Artist was being published. It was her great joy to share her published stories for others to read.

This book is also dedicated to the elders around the world who have yet to share their life stories.

Table of Contents

THE CELLAR DOOR

IN A WINDOW

BITS AND PIECES

Preface

Three Writers and an Artist came to me as many inspirations do: in a dream. One morning, in 2019, I awoke with a full vision of myself, and three friends, working together to create and publish a book. Not just any book. A book by three distinctly different writers and an artist.

Our voices are each unique. Our journeys, quite different. You will discover that like, the writers, each collection has a novel layout.

June Williams and Yvonne Finley have been creative writers, publishing or sharing their work for many years. While Sylvia Covington, a visual artist, had shifted away from fine art and for decades worked as a graphic designer. On the other hand, I have only written for work assignments. Additionally, we were all women of a 'certain age.'

Ultimately, **Three Writers and an Artist** symbolizes that no matter the age, you have a voice. There are lessons to be gleaned from our ever-expanding circle of elders. Some lessons are serious. Others are totally hilarious and nonsensical.

What I have learned as a woman of a 'certain age', is that my sentences and thoughts need not be perfect. We share our creative gifts never knowing how that ripple of creation will touch someone's life.   Linda RM Jones

The Cellar Door

June E. Williams

Curls hang down her back. bangs frame her face. No matter where she is: on the bus, a country road or, sitting with a dying friend- words find her: the girl with twist.

Educated for success, she spent time in Chicago, Ohio and New York City. Working her magic with children, fashion and as a government insider, -until bureaucratic and personnel nonsense sent her packing. Within months, she found that quiet place writers go, free and safe from harm.

From heart to hand her pencil races across the page, questioning everything she thought real, in contrast to reality, observing

through your eyes, and mine, life's unforeseen conditions.
She leans forward-my heart leaps!

I blush with excitement reading, in rhythm and rhyme her thoughtful, witty words, the healing moments, in "Notes from the Cellar Door."

James Bleu

THE CELLAR DOOR

The Collection

pink butterfly
it's personal
eternity
before the mayflower
red state blue state
urban rhymes
"who's foolin' who?"
the funeral
I hate the bus
the midnight ball
the foreigner is me!
flight 881
I should have known
when will you say my name
hit and run
at a glance
street corner hustle
street corner blues
bang bang 1976
southside bungalow
2190 days
this is not the neighborhood i left
revelation: for J & J

but you're the daughter
a colored man knows
L.A. & Mary: a conversation

pink butterfly

wearing a cape makes me think I can fly.

It's personal

it's easy telling people 'get over it, move on"

if you're not the one being 'fucked.'

eternity

unless there's life after death,
what's the purpose of your existence?
without knowing you were here?

before the mayflower

we don't always see us.
see everyone but, us.
sometimes the only us, in the room,
get mad if another us, comes in.

what a job they did
because they could on ...US.

red state, blue state

"the only thing Lincoln freed was himself"

red state... blue state
code words for confederate red; yankee blue:
the underbelly for American racism,
designed on purpose by political pundits,
with the puppet master's permission.

don't get it twisted, the civil war continues.

urban rhymes

how did 'sugar and spice and everything nice',
become "bitches and hoes" overnight?

or was it gradual?

a slow acceptance of cultural decline,
in venues we ascribe to,
choosing "freedom of speech"
over decency
greed over quality.

little by little we pattern ourselves,
by what we hear
what mainstream America considers okay.

conscience crumbles.
nothing is sacred.
our silent voices maintain the status quo,
irreverent at the sake of being.

who's foolin' who?"

education is the politician's whore.
promising dramatic changes for today's children.
once the election is over, so are the promises.
their children attend private or religious institutions
while yours, mine; Dick and Jane, sit in overcrowded classrooms,
with outdated books, lame teachers, paper pushing principals
and the engineer who runs the school.

baby Sally stays home, hoping Dick and Jane won't be shot.
if politicians placed the same emphasis, on education,
as they do their campaigns, no child would be left behind.

the funeral

taller than the tallest tree,
did you think I wouldn't know?
did you think I wouldn't feel you in the marrow of my bones?

soft, lovely,
wet, wild
bare naked bones,
did you think I wouldn't feel you in the seat of my soul?

you slay me
with your arrogance,
your wily smile
sly like a fox.

rode me on your back,
I didn't want to stop,

did you think I wouldn't know you were here?

"i hate the bus"

a bus filled with empty seats,
she sits next to me.

the bigger they are,
they sit next to me.

squeezed between two men,
i look across the aisle

"why would that woman put that old man's hat on that baby's
head?"

"no i don't have a fork," as the man who asked pulls from his bag,
a neatly wrapped plate and begins eating, using chicken
pieces as his utensils.

the passengers stare. the driver sees nothing.

i think i've seen it all until, a man raises his shirt, stabs himself with a
syringe,
closes his eyes knowing he'll see another day.

i hate the bus!

i hate the wheels going round and round, up and down, back and
forth, knocking passengers, in the arms and laps of strangers.

i hate the smell, the sound, people touching me,
me touching them; the stares i get as if on purpose.

PLEASE!!

read your book. hold your phone "the heartbeat of your life."
plug your ears.
keep your baby quiet...
and the dog you carry from barking.

i hate the bus!

i hate what i see. what i hear.
the wanna be girls, who wanna be boys,
who don't want to be men.

i hate the improper behavior. the language.

"i have trouble hearing my own voice;" why would i want
to hear yours.

or, see your dragging pants, showing your underwear.

i hate the meowing heard in back; i'm allergic to cats.

i hate the driver exchange, the howdy-do's when in a hurry.

i hate the winter snow, the freezing rain: the sweltering summer sun.

the wait seems forever; i'm glad when you come.

i hate that i hate.... BUT...I DO.

the midnight ball

who wouldn't want
a boys beautifully bagged lunch,
a woman's red soled shoes,
a girls iPad,
her father's Escalade?

who among us hasn't peeked
through a keyhole, looked over a fence,
envious of what we see, breaking the tenth commandment, with
our insatiable appetites, creating an environment of thugs,
deviates, in
house traders, burglars, bank fraud, sex for hire, drugs on demand?

come one, come all
to **the midnight ball**,
the trophy can be yours...
if the price is right?

we are a filmmaker's delight,
art in its truest form,
living the characters out loud.

the foreigner is me!

on the bus
in a cab
on the train
in the air:
land where our fathers died
hanging from trees,
fighting for freedom,
marching for peace...
no one speaks English,
the foreigner is me!

flight 881

riding scared, on the back of a scooter,
hair blowing in the breeze, warmed by the Thailand sun.

seeing sights, hearing sounds,
eating mangos off trees,

while Buddhist monks make their way through narrow streets,
cobbled stone sidewalks,

merchants buying and selling goods,
shepherds tending their flock.

children playing soccer,
and God said, "let there be rain."

i thought it would never end.

i am the American grandmother,
the silent song,
they didn't see 'til now

i should have known

love can be so complicated: it doesn't conquer all.
 sorry I wasn't it. sorry?
i should have known.
i should have listened to my head, not my heart.
i should have run when i could, when my shoes were brand new,

when you couldn't catch me.
how convincing you were.
i believed.

i believed the star we wished upon "til it fell at my feet
i will lick my wounds, while the music plays,
while my heart laughs, while i can still dance.
i should have known.

when will you say my name?

i sit, in the fifth row, second seat,
next to the window.
i sit next to the boy who picks his nose,
the girl who can't sit still.
i wear BLUE every day except, THURDAYS.
i answer questions, in my head,
my hand goes UNNOTICED.
how can you teach me?
if you don't know i'm here?
When will you say my name?

with hand on heart,
i pledge allegiance to the flag.
answering questions in my head.
you give me CRUMBS,
expecting BREAD.
WHen will you say my name?

WHEn will you see the girl, in BLUE,
out of breath, with worn out shoes,
dodgin' bullets, in the neighborhood,
next to the boy who looks like you.

how will you know what's in my head?

21

today, is THURSDAY i'm wearing RED.

you see me not.
I see you still.
WHEN WILL YOU SAY MY NAME?

hit and run

don't wait
for the absentee parent
to be any more
than what they are...
absent.

at a glance

at any given time, around any given corner.
i am he that is she.
begging bread.
looking for shelter.
a place to lay my head.

you turn away.
not without cause, whisper to your neighbor;
as though i'm not there.
the me that is she,
could also be you...

at any given time, around any given corner.

street corner hustle

loose squares,
loose squares
loose women
loose men
loose lips

kiss and tell,

"the iceman cometh"

love for sell.

street corner BLUES

blank face

white tee's

low hanging pants,

lean against the sky

masked with despair.

bang! bang!

1976

scattered pictures cover the dead man's body, near the cellar door
an obvious hit by someone who knew the evidence would
expose government officials engaged in illicit sex with female
employees.
someone who knew what i couldn't prove.

Truth, nor fear, would no longer hold me hostage so i left;
taking my dreams but, not far enough before,
the Chicago police knocked on my door requesting i call the chief
who knew my story.

the officials were fired.
the killer never found,
and my life changed forever.

what a grand disappointment!

southside bungalow, 1978

truth unravels mind

pain subsides

will survives

in the house Jack built.

2190 days

i lie awake,
in a small sterile town-
white walls,
white wine,
white people.

absent of myself,
where no one comes, not even God.

sallow is my skin.
my hair turning gray.
wearing shoes that pinch my toes-
shoes that walk me slow.

when will this nightmare end?

the lonely days of summer.
the winter of my tears.

this is not the neighborhood i left

this is not the neighborhood I left.
what land did you furrow?
what grain did you mill?
what cotton did you pick?
what whip crossed your back?

the country that let you in kept us out.
you get what we can't.
you have free reign, free access.
what you take from us,
you don't give back.

this is not the neighborhood i left.

revelation: for J & J

the world is full of painted faces.

like clowns, in yesterday's parade

marching to a tune that has no sound.

a beat that has no drum.

What happened to my laughter?

but you're the daughter

what i'm doing is not who i am--a wounded child.
sitting crossed legged on the floor watching her,
watch me through an open bathroom door.

hoping she will hurry fast.
so i can... wipe, bathe, wash, clean, in her home.
uprooted from mine.
travel together in time.
a changed time.
a different time.

her husband gone,
the son away.
except for me ...the chosen one.
pre-ordained at birth.

How can this be?
"sons and lovers"
come and go.
wipe a brow, hold a hand.

Wasn't it a man, Jesus gave his mother to?

a colored man knows....

the preacher knew,

the professor didn't.

and the 'accidental tourist' living in the white house,

(when the giant couldn't keep him out) is learning...

...what a colored man is in a white man's eyes.

L.A. & Mary: a conversation

L.A.: there's a wind change, a shift in the atmosphere.
"mo' niggas" are coming home from prison, than college.
more young black males emulate the prison behavior,
glamorized by the media, using music and film as their
backdrop. the sugar and spice girl wants the 'thug,' not
the book carrying, suit wearing, intelligent gent.

Mary: it's all by design. the same way they mis-educate our
Children, they mis-educate the world about who we are.
there's no balance in how we're portrayed. a black
president is a distorted perception of America's racial reality.

L.A.: where do we go from here? what happens next for us? for
them?

Mary: ask Uncle Sugar. weren't you there when he
came to town? when he passed out dreams? we got the
leftovers, the "hand me downs,"
the "audacity to hope" wasn't allowed.

In A Window Out A Window
Linda RM Jones

Reliable. Resourceful.
Creative. Insightful.
She makes a mean pot of
greens.

From the hills of West Virginia
to Chicago's busy streets.
An author and collector.
She always aims to please.

An advocate for women,

She does everything with ease.
Gives voice to truth.

A mystery she is...

Poetry in motion, Not easily impressed.
She sets a table for Kings and Queens
Around her latest whim.

The Collection

38

Wood Nymph

In the forest under the trees sits
a wood nymph, sexy and free.
Whistling a melody light as a breeze
hoping in time to be touched, loved by me.

Dancing to music unheard but to her.
The wood nymph moves gracefully, sexy and free.
Touched by a breeze, not yet by me.

Floating on the water, kissed by the sun
wood nymphs gather to play and have fun.

Wood nymphs' parade through a valley lush green.
Flowers strewn high, decorate trees.
Birds gather quickly hearing the whistle

My wood nymph is dying, there is no breeze.
Stuffed in a box full of dead people. Not freed.
Reaching for the wood nymph ---
Caught a finger ---
Touched her.
She is me.

In the Beginning There Was Man

Well, Not Quite

Woman was bored and asked God for a toy.

She said to woman. "You need a mate, a companion, someone who will stimulate you. Then God laughed.

"But I simply want a toy. Something to entertain me when I am bored".

God began to laugh again, and She spoke gently to woman saying.
"You shall have a toy, a mate and a companion in one. I shall call it man".

He shall be your toy, something to amuse you.
He shall be a mate and companion. Someone who can help you
and provide for you.
Someone who will protect you.

As a woman you are like me, a great creative mind force, a giver, and nurturer of life and the
embodiment of all that is possible.
You are a complete reflection of all that I am.

40

'Man shall do all things necessary for your greater comfort and pleasure".

So, spoke God in the very beginning to her creation... whom she called woman.

Knowing

I met you through the eyes of a man claiming to know
you.
He wrote about your personal relationships as if they
were mysteries
of badges bestowed on you from an unknown source for
a long
deceased reason.

In 1938, in a southern city you died. Today, experts
debate over 'how',
from an all-white hospital refusing to admit you',
or from 'severe loss of blood'.

Neither argument matters.
I know the truth.

Others introduced me to you on stage-singing and
drinking.
At first, I believed it was you but no,
only a shadow with fragments.

Columbia records proclaims it has saved you for the
world

by releasing an entire collection of your music bringing you back
to the world some forty years after your death.

I still found only a shadow.

One day I heard a bellowing bluesy sound.
A wail of sparking spectacular sounds of pain, love and loss
pierced the ears of my soul.

You were there!

Sitting on the bar stool caressing a glass.
Nursing it as a lover not yet lost.

How could it be you?

We met one autumn day.

Your anger swept me from your path.
Rage propels you to rule your world.
Insecurity causes a seeking of companionship and recognition from peers.

I've watched you in business meetings, social gatherings,

love affairs and in my mirror.

Did you die on that highway? I know the truth.
You, Bessie Smith, are alive.

Every note slipping past your lips reflects parts of our
lives.
A pain from living a life of rejection laced with a
bittersweet
perception of ourselves.

You were not afraid to show the pain.

Today, we hide.

All pain is wrapped in sophistication, an illusion of
acceptance.
Bluesy notes bellow behind closed doors,
while liquor is consumed in genteel fashion.

Singing of lost men, happy, and sad, moments evoke
response
but-may not cause tears until doors close.

Your/Our mystery of life was, and is, a badge of
courage, determination,
and deep-seated strength, splashed with humor and
dappled with love.

This was/is you/us.

I know - The Empress of the blues still lives behind closed doors and closing hearts of Black women, walking the earth with torches of rejection-confusion.

Hoping the flame finally flickers then glows bright with love.

You were us. We are you.

A New Word for Chris

Pondering my path in life a word occurred to me.
It symbolized the choices that I make. Throughout my life path,
which I sought, was that of an Ant, not a Grasshopper.

It is most true and very wise to recognize that what you
deny is truly you.

Do not misunderstand, I am like an Ant, very industrious,
sampling life and selecting what is good and taking it home.
As best I can, I prepare for tomorrow. Does he enjoy life? Of course.
How industrious is an Ant and how much life does it enjoy?

What about a Grasshopper? Grasshoppers do not work.
They toil only for their personal pleasure. They eat, play in the flowers,
and make no preparations for tomorrow. That is not me, or is it?

The grasshopper takes pleasure in life at every turn.

That is like purchasing five bags of cookies when only
one was required.
Like the Grasshopper resting and eating on a leaf, you
eat a bag of cookies in a day.

For eating is a pleasure.

Am I a Grasshopper or an Ant, maybe neither?

More like a Tortoise, slowly moving through life,
observing everything.
Does a Tortoise enjoy life in slow motion? Of course. It
knows no other life.
A Tortoise is never exhausted, like the too busy, quick
moving Hare.

Hmmm, sometimes the Tortoise is too slow. Do not
misunderstand,
the Tortoise gets its goal. But how much more life could
have
been observed with just a little more speed?

Now the Hare is either, moving quick or lounging,
watching, and listening to life.
For me, that lounging, watching, and listening part
sounds great.

The Hare never appears to be concerned about the next moment. Life is Now!

This brings me back to the beginning, well not quite. You see I have discovered that I am a **Torgrasanthar** (tor-gra-san-thar)©.

You will not find that in your trusty Webster's. Simply put, Torgrasanthar© is a mix of a Tortoise, Grasshopper, Ant, and a Hare.

A Torgrasanthar© is a person who deliberately moves through life, enjoying every moment in balance. Taking no heed to tomorrow, while putting aside a portion of every moment to share with those along the way.

What an exciting new word.

TORGRASANTHAR! ©

Changed not Changed

I have changed.

I really have not.
Only re-submerged as reflections of
that which is really me.

The me nobody knows.
Everyone who knew me,
Really knew me.

Only I did not know.

Can You Find Your Way?

Loneliness wraps you.
Darkness - hides all light.
People pass never seeing.
Never seeing pain.
Your pain.
Pain of loss.
All is in memory.
Memory flows - with the
unbroken life of the Universe.

In the Evening

In the evening of your days a moment
of peace consumes you.
Daylight fades into twilight and order
surrounds you.
Life is a whirl - devoid of silences.
That is today.
What will be
tomorrow?

Here Sit I

Here Sit I!
A wandering spirit.
Drifting from moment to moment.

Ever thinking.
Not so clearly.
What am I about?
Sitting, ever sitting.
Standing, ever standing.

Do I move from point to point?
Or hover as a bee.
Hoping that this is the flower
with pollen meant for me.

Do Little is my name.
Dreaming is my game.

T

T   is for Touching, Teasing,
     Tenderly near you.

Touching I hold you.
Teasingly warm you.

T is for Tomorrow.
When you will Touch
    Teasingly
Tenderly Love Me.

Man Is

Doctors thinking illness
Causing illness-
Curing illness-
Giving medicine-
patented death.

Children dying.

Women and men -
thinking illness-
causing illness-
Curing illness.

Man is now an Illness!

Man speaks of life
yet prescribes death,
sees death-
fears death-
runs from death.

Death-
Man's unavoidable companion.

We Watch

We watch – life changes.
Each moves into his own illusion.
One wanting time not to share responsibilities of others.
Having today totally to himself.

Life cannot be that way.
All are connected.
Each must help the other.
One gives, the other gives.

Then each can take always sharing.
Knowing all creations are unions of both.
Watch as life changes.
Causing each to move into his own illusion.

Now I Lay Me Down

Now I lay me
down to sleep
knowing the Lord
my soul will keep.

I thank the Lord
for the blessings and
lessons of this day.

Knowing and trusting
that tomorrow
when I awake
the Lord will
lead me
on my way.

In a Window Out a Window

Apple, cherries, peaches, pears, and plums
Flowers fragrant heavily in the air.
Running down dirt roads
Touching snapdragons, holly hocks, and roses.

In a window
Out a window
Flowers dangling over walls.

Announcing spring in all its glory
Milk weed hosting butterflies
Poke weed yielding purple berries
Black walnut hanging on the trees.

In a window
Out a window
On the upper porch
Jumping rope, Jacks, Pick-up sticks,

Apples, cherries, peaches, pears, and plums.

In A Window - Out a Window
Running down dirt roads.

Bits and Pieces

Yvonne Finley

My soul doth give glory to my great and mighty God and
greatly exalts praises upon His holy name – for He has
wrought wonders upon me who has come from poor,
obscure and uncared for places.

He hath made me – a barren woman—the joyful mother
of three children. He entrusted me the task of guiding,
molding and leading to His temple.
He has blessed and enabled me to share lean resources. He
has given
me wisdom to glean,
sufficient resources(money) to make a way for us.

He has been a Waymaker when there seemed to be no way.
He has provided shelter in times of storm and empowered me
to share His
love with other wayfarers in need of comfort.

I will shout His praises forever more and share his
provisions as his steward feeble earthenware vessel that
I am fleshed in holy blackness.
Magnificat by Yvonne Finley

BITS and PIECES

The Collection

The May-September Affair
Promises Promises
Alma, Will You Give Me Another Cup of Coffee?
Paper, Trees, Books
The Day Daddy Ate the Duck
Black Magic
Black on Black Love
My Piano Tuner
I'm Going Through

The May - September Affair

Jake fancied himself a dashing Romeo. He and Sue Ellen, a wisp of a young girl, sat in his dusty, ancient truck, used for hauling hay. They were on the outskirts of town, at dusk, on an August Friday evening.

Jake nervously said, "Sue Ellen, why don't we just take off and go, 150 miles, to Yucca Flats? I can't marry you right now, but we could set up a house. My friend, Roy, has a ranch and I could give him a hand. How about it, baby girl?" Sue Ellen's eyes widened, and she said in a shocked voice "Jake, you must be crazy!" She was longing to go to the picture show. Then later sneak a couple of drinks before returning home to her boring uneventful teenage life. She had gotten involved with Jake for a summer adventure, an affair with an older man, just to see if she could lead him on. Here he goes talking bull crap about living together. Jake was still talking in a torrent of words, but Sue Ellen tuned him out.

She was thinking about what color nail polish to try Saturday at the beauty parlor. Sue Ellen dreams of living in some faraway city as a sophisticated lady wearing fancy dresses and enjoying herself. She has no intention of permanently hitching up with a middle-aged, going to seed farmer, as old as her daddy. Men were funny: one roll or so in the hay, and they confess to undying love.

Finally, hearing Jake say they could drive to Yucca Flats she states, "I can't leave my family. No way for another Hicksville. If you can't take me to the show and let things, be like they are then drive me to Dyers Road so I can go home."

Jake was jolted back to reality. He put his hand in his pocket and brings out a small box handing it to Sue Ellen. "Baby girl, this is a special present for you." Excitedly Sue Ellen accepts and opens the box. In it lay a small 14k gold charm bracelet with the #1. Jake usually not a man of many words quietly says, "Gal, I want you to always know that you are #1 in my heart and never settle for nothing but the best." Jake fastens the bracelet on Sue Ellen's wrist. She gives him a spontaneous kiss and a sincere "Thanks."

Jake and Sue Ellen drove 10 miles in silence back to Dyers Road. At the road to her house, Sue Ellen jumped out, turned, smiled, and waved. She set off resolutely for home and her next adventure. Jake ruefully realized that the affair with a girl the age of his daughter, Kay, was over. The romance had lasted the three months of summer. As he watches Sue Ellen's figure retreating, his mind turns to home and the back fence that needs repairing and a wife that had been neglected for a long time.

He wondered how he could've been fool enough to want to run away with a young girl. Backing the truck out onto the main road, he hopes his wife, Melinda, has whipped up a tasty dinner of smothered pork chops, gravy, rice, and homemade biscuits, as he was famished after this escapade. Silently, he smokes a Camel cigarette, inhaling the smoke, thankful that he had come to his senses. Eagerly, he put his foot on the gas, pushing his old truck to get home. He hopes that nobody, but Melinda knows he has been an old fool.

Promises, Promises

The American dream of owning a business is no longer a reality. In the late nineteen forties, the American economy was booming. Small mom and pop businesses flourished in the neighborhoods, in an age of free enterprise. An individual with cash and a lot of sweat equity could start a corner grocery, or hardware store, and expect to operate a successful independent business while earning a comfortable living.

In the nineteen nineties, depending on the state of your wallet the economy was in either a recession or a depression. The government was liberally offering small business loans. Now even the welfare mother could acquire a loan to start a small business in her low rent apartment nearly as easily as she can organize a Tupperware party.

The big question is what chance of success has she, a welfare mother, or anyone else who borrows operating money? Can she possibly be even close to having a stable business on sound financial footing a year from its inception, regardless of how hard she works and with insufficient business acumen? The chance is practically nil from my observation.

The South end of the Chicago Loop where I worked in 1978 was once a flourishing business section. It has become a ghost of its former vitality. Stores like Montgomery Ward, Wieboldt's, Chas. A. Stevens, Goldblatt's, Hillman's Fine

Foods and Sears are gone. Other, countless, small businesses that sprouted on major streets like Jackson, Adams and State disappeared nearly overnight. With mergers, cutbacks and takeovers affecting big business, what chance does Joe Blow or Mr. Average Citizen, have of successfully operating a small business?

I have a middle-aged neighbor, both he and his wife are teachers. They opened two separate, small, neighborhood businesses. After working long hours, both businesses folded. I wonder if the investment in the businesses could have been better invested in a savings bond, I.R.A. account or college fund for their children. It now seems that for every successful Mary Kay Enterprise, nine or more small businesses go bankrupt.

I personally think an individual who has never shot a gun has a greater chance of going on safari and bagging a leopard than small businesses stand a chance of succeeding.

The middle and lower classes are joining the disenfranchised. It seems only "old money" and Savings and Loan companies can secure risk-free government loans and flourish. Maybe we need to invoke President Hoover's ghost and settle for his promise of a chicken in every pot!

What happened to a "kinder, gentler America?"

Alma, Will You Give Me Another Cup of Coffee?

I'm Joe, one of the few old-time regulars left in this neighborhood café on the south-side of Chicago. We old timers have seen many changes on East 63rd Street. While this part of town once bustled with traffic, booming businesses, and industry --- almost like the downtown area, or loop… it is dying.

We fellas had such high hopes that it would always be like it used to be. We were young, brash, and fresh out of World War II. We got married, bought homes, and raised families. We were contributors to our communities, with our union jobs and saving accounts. We were the Black bourgeois.

We felt like we had a gold mine. The years went by, our kids grew up and went to college. We were getting older and one day the economy died for us. Our jobs closed, moved to the Sun Belt, or foreign countries.

We woke up to be old, broke down and poor with no more opportunity. Some of the guys gave up, died of heart attacks or cancer but it was really broken hearts.

A few of us survivors keep an optimistic front. We read the newspaper and hope for better days again.

To maintain a daily routine, we gather together to drink coffee. We mask our anger and despair with a smile putting on a brave front.

You can almost smell the despair in this almost abandoned, decrepit area. The neighborhood cafe is our island for lost, old souls. Business is always slow however we have friendship. We often reminisce like an old hound dog sleeping by the fireplace, dreaming of hunting rabbits.

We live on small pensions. Alma, the waitress-owner, has come to terms with her own broken dreams. She treats us like her disillusioned children.

"Alma, how about another cup of coffee, sweetheart?"

Doggedly, in her weariness, she passes it deftly with no comment. She looks bone tired. Like us, she is old, broke down, and poor with no more opportunity or dreams to vitalize her.

69

Paper, Trees, Books

In the old movie, Black Orpheus, an elderly man tells the frantic Orpheus that he will not find Eurydice in the archaic massive old building that looks like a tomb. He says, "There is only paper here. She is not here". There were floors and floors of paper stored in the building and for what purpose? No one seemed to read it.

Those words recall the situation in many office buildings in Chicago business areas. All over the world as a matter of fact, there is storage of tons of paper.

We have removed millions and millions of trees, every year, to make paper of all types and descriptions. We are decimating our earth and many times being extravagant and grossly wasteful.

We need to replenish our earth as lovingly as we manufacture paper. We need to read the books that already exist and use the knowledge to benefit and transform our world.

I love books, like Johnny Appleseed, planted trees everywhere. I lovingly share by giving away books to touch someone's life.

Our earth's resources continue to diminish. Mother Earth struggles to sustain us. I am ever cognizant that every printed book, note card, kitchen and bathroom paper item came originally from a living tree. I recycle items as much as possible to further conserve energy thereby reducing my carbon footprint.

The gorges in Africa and systematic elimination of the Rain Forest in South America saddens me. It moves me to support the 'Green Peace Movement' by authorizing a withdrawal from my sparse funds to aid our ailing earth. My resolve, like Johnny Appleseed, is to live simply, plant a small tree in my back yard, conserve energy and work to educate others to plant trees, seeds, donate and recycle books.

The Day Daddy Ate the Duck

(A true story)

Daddy called me, his first-born daughter, 'string bean' in my early years. When mother and Nanny were peeved with me, they said that I looked like my father. I did resemble him. Daddy was debonair and handsome and smoked a pipe. Daddy was an avid, fluent, reader and proud that I loved books. By the same token, he was short on patience when I had trouble with arithmetic.

I quickly learned Daddy could not slay dragons to protect me. When, at the age of two, dressed in a white wool sweater with tassels around the collar I witnessed a family crisis. Nanny pulled a gun on Daddy while I was in his arms to prevent him from taking me out of her house. As I fell to the floor I looked up and asked him, "Why did you drop me?" Daddy was too scared to answer. He quickly left leaving me stunned and calling his name. The gun incident set the stage for Daddy's Sunday visit years later.

We lived with Nanny, our great aunt, in a small three-room, cold water flat. It was a female centered household. Paul, known to our family as "Brother", and I basked in male attention whenever Daddy, or our uncles came to visit. We would be ecstatic to receive fragments of a male's time and attention, especially Daddy's.

It was a picture perfect bright sunny Easter in April. The day was so beautiful, like one of Nanny's postcards, especially to an inquisitive six-year-old first grader. My brother, Paul, was five years old. It was a lazy warm afternoon after mass and things were boring. Suddenly, there was a pounding on the door. Mother opened it and there stood Daddy.

Paul and I were elated that Daddy had come to bring his weekly check. At age two, following the gun incident, my parents were divorced. Normally, he mailed his weekly support check or sent it by one of his many girlfriends.

After their bitter divorce, mother had very little patience with Daddy. On this Easter Sunday mother led us to the kitchen and sat us at the table. Quickly mother left returning to the living room. Nanny was visiting our next-door neighbor. It was just Daddy and his two children, alone at the kitchen table.

This was a rather lengthy Easter Sunday visit. Daddy reviewed some of my homework and listened while I read a favorite story. Finally, he helped me with arithmetic, the one subject with which I struggled. This time Daddy gave me a long intense lecture, saying that there is no such word as "can't." His words and message have never been forgotten.

Nanny and my mother prepared big meals on Sunday, which was a Southern tradition. This being Easter, we were having a special meal. Wonderful smells of the cooking filled the kitchen. Dinner included homemade buttery rolls and blueberry cobbler. The staple and star of our meal was mother's delicious succulent, crispy brown duck. Mother was cooling this special treat on the far end of the kitchen table, near the wall away from us.

Daddy must have been overcome with hunger pangs, as the kitchen was full of smells of good food, or he was nostalgic for our mother's cooking. Daddy knew Nanny was absent, so he did not have to fear for his life. The carving knife was within reach. On impulse Daddy decided to sneak a piece of the duck. He engaged us in a low running dialogue of questions and answers. Continuing in his charming fashion he wove an exciting story while he maneuvered the knife. So, entranced in the story were we, that we did not sound the alarm or yell for our mother.

He ate tiny bits quickly without interrupting the flow of conversation with us. My five-year-old brother, who was always hungry, was so captivated that he never noticed. Daddy did not share any tidbits of the duck. I don't know how Brother let Daddy eat without sharing with him. We were content because we were going to have a good Sunday dinner as usual. It didn't dawn on us that the major ingredient was in Daddy's stomach.

Daddy was so skilled with the knife that when he finished there was only a carcass with the bones intact. Finally, when Daddy was preparing to leave, he must have looked guilty, or smug, like a sly old fox caught in the hen house red-handed. My mother noticed the platter and the skeleton where her duck had reigned in royal splendor.

She screamed like a banshee and voiced a few strong cuss words not meant for tender ears. But in our small quarters, we had heard them before and knew Mama was very, very angry. Daddy, usually so assertive, retreated like a guilty crest fallen puppy who had wet the rug. He may have tried to issue an apology, "I didn't mean to eat the whole thing."

Later, we ate salmon croquettes with the rest of the regal dinner. The aroma of regal duck wafted through the house and down through the years in my memory. I don't think Mama ever cooked a duck again.

Black Magic

A Black Man
A Black Woman

A look
A touch
A hug
A kiss

Ecstasy

Somethings can't be discovered in books!

Black on Black Love

A kind of quiet

A kind of Calm

A playful quality and quiet laughter

Intense passion that can be unfurled
A peacefulness and fun in the relationship
Quiet talks in the middle of the night
An appreciation of one for the other

An awe about the power and beauty of it all
An earthiness about it all
What a joy, What a magic, What an attraction!

Gee Whiz

My Piano Tuner

Growing up in my family the lesson demonstrated was that strong women need strong men in their lives. It's a yin/yang type of thing for wholeness.

It's something about a male's appreciative glance or smile that can make a virtuous female strut her stuff and feel a bit more special in her feminine unique powers. It was such a relationship that really affirmed me.

The relationship began following the demise of an eighteen-year marriage. The relationship grew out of a friendship and its essence was communication. I did not define myself through David's eyes but grew and had fun.

David was a creative man - a musician, at home with himself. He was mature and had his own space. He was seasonal like clockwork; he was around from October to April. He was the bear, and I was the cave. This went on for eight years until I was ready for a different, amiable relationship. I grew in the ability to love myself, not settle for crumbs, and be whole.

I can be tender and open, warm, and emphatic, but as an ancient one, I do not define my womanish powers by the mandate of a male partner. I have peace with myself. I can enjoy aloneness and solitude. I welcome friends into my world, but do not define myself by their presence or absence.

Like relishing a jelly doughnut, I appreciate a chance encounter with a sensitive man while eating a delicious meal in a restaurant. Enjoying a casual yet stimulating male/female conversation before venturing forth alone into the night.

I consider myself too special to be a trophy woman or one of many women in a man's pursuit of pleasure and sensual delight. If a man would commit to a monogamous relationship, had sensitivity, a willingness to grow and explore his mid-life self, I might be interested. But in the meantime…I'll remember what has been and forge on alone, not lonely, but fulfilled with males in limited capacities in my life.

I'm on a mission of self-discovery. Women fore- bearers, strong and anchored are my role models, Anna Julia Cooper, Sojourner Truth, Fannie Barrier Williams, Lorraine Hansberry, Mary McCloud Bethune, Audre Lorde, Ida B. Wells, Maya Angelou, Lena Horne, and Cicely Tyson. They are my guides - no wilting lilies standing in male shadows.

After my encounter with David, my Piano Tuner, I emerged still bi-polar but stabilized, whole and a strong Black woman in love with life.

I'm Going Through

Difficult times and problems will not slay me
I'm going through.
Times may be rough and solutions not immediately at hand
But - I'm going through.
Times may be unsteady and answers only remotely discerned
But I'm going through.

I have come too far to be turned around. I have prayed far too
Long to be dismayed.
The bottom line - as strong as my heart's conviction
Can make it is - I'm going through.

My God who holds tomorrow in His hand and will allow me
To hold the edge of His garment,
My God will lead the way, and I can state with heart felt
conviction - -
No doubt of His love which is like pure gold -
My God and I are going through.

My faith may get a little tattered and ragged at the edges, but
then
He touched me ever so gently and with Faith aglow and joy in
my soul -

Gently, I take up my cross and go through.

AFTERWORDS

Three Writers

Interviews

~June Williams~

Question: What was your first love, reading or writing?

JW: Reading was by far my first love.

Question: How did you develop into a writer?

JW: Writing came naturally to me. In the first or second grade my poem, "My Christmas Wish," was published in the December issue of the McCosh Magnet, the school paper. My mother saved the 1949 publication.

Question: What inspires your writing?

JW: So many things. Sometimes the smallest thing, a spoken or seen word, even an event. Just living inspires me to express in words my response. A lot of times in the silence I hear the words.

Question: What attracted you to this book project?

JW: The vision of the women writers, our individual stories, and the unique layout to share our stories sparked my interest. Women were the highlight, and it was exciting. Three women being together spoke to my spirit. Since Phyllis Wheatley, black women writers have used their voices to capture the essence of American culture. From Maya Angelou to Nikki Giovanni, Carolyn Rogers to Alice Walker, their dual viewpoints and various genre endured through critical pressure. Like these women before us we were being asked to speak our truth, however that is with humor and warmth, without strain or distortion but, with the presence of grace.

Question: Speaking of spirit, what is your spirit animal?

JW: Oh, the noble deer. Throughout my life in various places and incidents a deer has appeared. It often feels like they are nudging or guiding me in a direction or even a feeling. I have learned to be observant when I sense the deer presence.

Question: What is the best advice you'd give your younger self?

JW: So many things I would say. Life is not a neatly wrapped package tied with a bow. It's everything but ... step lightly and with care. Being a mother is a mother ... know what you are doing. Who said you want to be a mother anyway? Beware of the two-legged wolf in suits, ties, pantyhose, and high heel shoes. That is my advice to my younger self.

Question: How do you identify happiness at this stage of your life?

JW: With all the challenges in today's world my answer is very simple. Happiness is feeling good.

~Linda RM Jones~

Question: What was your first love reading or writing:

LRMJ: Oh dear, I absolutely dread writing. I love reading. My earliest clear memory is sitting with my mother, and she is reading Bambi to me. My favorite book to read as a child was <u>Miss</u> <u>Pattie</u>. That book and two others, where the first books I received at age 7, and are still in my library today. Being able to read and explain a children 's versions of Shakespeare at age 12 kept me from being demoted when I transferred to catholic school. So, reading remains my first love.

Question: You did say you dread writing. So how did you develop into a writer?

LRMJ: First off, I do not consider myself a writer. I write through sheer pain and torture. It is fascinating to see your thoughts on paper, but the process for me is fraught with criticism and rejection. Academically, my writing skills were always criticized in negative ways. In high school, both my catholic and public-school experience were with white women who loved red ink. Although, my thoughts were on the page there were always technical errors. As an adult, I have spent years working in positions that require me to write. From college papers, public relation projects, non-profit grants, board of director reports, and educational materials, I learned to write. But the greatest thing I learned is the value of editors they make sure I have met the worlds standards and expectations. So, I write.

Questions: Describe what it feels like to accomplish publishing a

83

book of your own?

LRMJ: It is exciting because I set a goal, stayed the course, fought my fears of failure, and conquered the challenge. Simultaneously, it is overwhelming because once people find out you are writing a book or have a book being published their expectations are voiced as if they should be your expectations. Yet, once you have the book in your hand it is exciting and gratifying to see your name and title on the cover. No matter what happens with the book I think more people should share the joy of seeing their name on their own written creation.

Question: What is your spirit animal?

LRMJ: I've never thought about a spiritual animal but in my home, there are several hares and some rabbits. Now they are not the same animal. I really like hares and will purchase the long eared and long footed creatures whenever I find them. But you find more rabbits, so I have both. So, I am choosing the Hare as my spirit animal.

Question: What is the best advice you'd give your younger self?

LRMJ: Keep developing your skills. Over the years I've accepted many different jobs. Therefore, my talents are very diverse, and my experiences create a foundation for my growth. Not just writing skills. Everything you do helps create who you become, and you are always becoming. Officially, I am retired but I am still becoming. As long as you are breathing you are becoming. My best advice is to keep growing, keep developing you and never stop moving through life becoming more you every moment.

Question: How do you identify happiness at this stage of your life?

LRMJ: First off, waking up is the most grateful moment every day. Then being able to recognize that my mind is still functioning, and my body is still able to naturally move and fully function. Then happiness is hearing my husband puttering around the house, or knowing he is reading in our sunroom. Happiness is always getting a daily check in call from my daughter. Part of my happiness at this age is sharing time and good moments with my sisters, cousins, and girlfriends. Happiness is living my best life at all moments.

~Yvonne Finley~

Question: What was your first love reading or writing?

YF: I loved them both. My mother and Aunt would give me books, pencil, and paper as a toddler. That is how I learned to read and write. Writing and reading has always been part of my life.

Question: Do you feel there is a spirit animal reflective of your life journey and if so, why?

YF: Several years ago, I was told the Wolf was my spirit animal. My understanding is that the wolf guides and protects as you journey on new unexplored paths. The wolf also symbolizes conquering deep fears and learning to journey with confidence. Knowing those aspects alone reflects my life so the wolf does symbolize my journey.

Question: You have mentioned that you began writing as a young child. What continues to inspire you today as a writer?

YF: There are various current events such as the recent 2020 protest and social disturbances. Mostly my inspiration is writing family history vignettes. These are brief sharing's for my daughter and grandchildren primarily concerning members of my mother's family.

Question: Why do you feel it is important to write stories about your ancestors and various relatives?

YF: African Americans constantly see and hear about the lives and successes of other people and cultures that do not look like us or share our unique American experience. For example, the Old Testament is about Jewish history. African Americans in general believe those old Jewish ancestors did not look anything like us or that their stories are about our ancestors on the African continent. American history is very much from the white Anglo-Saxon Protestant view. So, for me it is important that my family know our story.

Question: Please share a little about your family story.

YF: My great grandfather, Milton Springfield, was from Brownsville, Tennessee. He was not a minister but helped to establish Methodist churches in Tennessee. He was also a founding member of Lane College. He believed in freedom and education. Several family members left Tennessee. Milton's granddaughters, Horty B., Ester Lee, and Etta D. Springfield were in Indianapolis, Indiana. There they owned and operated the 3 Sisters Nursing Home. According to family records this business began in the late 1940s and remained in operation until the late 1990s. It is important to let the young know that our families have been in various successful businesses. Living as a descendant of slavery in America is a

challenge but we are survivors. My prayer, and goal, is to leave my history to help us continue building our families and communities.

Question: What attracted you to this book project?

YF: Just the idea of seeing my work in a book was exciting. Knowing that my daughter and grandchildren would have something from me in book form is very satisfying.

Question: How do you identify happiness at this stage of your life?
YF: As you know I am bi-polar, and I know that everyday can be challenging. But I continue to awake. With each moment I'm awake I thank God and cycle through any temporary bi-polar challenge. Being alive is happiness.

The Index

The Cellar Door

June E. Williams

The Index cont.

In a Window Out a Window
Linda RM Jones

The Index cont.

Bits and Pieces

Yvonne Finley

www.ingramcontent.com/pod-product-compliance
Lightning Source LLC
Chambersburg PA
CBHW061524050726
47503CB00016B/2726